T0071078

# THE POCKET GUIDE TO FIELD DRESSING, BUTCHERING, AND COOKING DEER

## A HUNTER'S QUICK REFERENCE BOOK

Monte and Joan Burch

First Skyhorse Publishing edition 2015



Visit our website at www.skyhorsepublishing.com.

10 9 8

Library of Congress Cataloging-in-Publication Data is available on file.

Cover design by Brian Peterson
Cover illustration: Thinkstock

Print ISBN: 978-1-63450-450-8
Ebook ISBN: 978-1-63450-468-3

Printed in China

# CONTENTS

# INTRODUCTION

To many hunters, the joy of the hunt stops when the deer is down. Many inexperienced deer hunters often look at dressing and butchering as hard,

complicated work requiring special tools, skills, and knowledge. The job also appears messy and smelly. Actually, field dressing, butchering, and cooking venison is quite easy. It can be done by the first-timer with very little hassle if done properly. Learning the proper steps and doing them in order prevents problems. This book lists all the steps in order in an easy-to-read manner with full illustrations. It can be used right in the field, allowing even the first-timer to enjoy the satisfaction of preparing his own venison. Old timers may also discover some new tricks.

# 1. YOUR DEER IS DOWN

The quality of your venison begins with proper care in the field.

The hunt is over and your deer is down. The first step is to make sure the animal is dead. Approach the animal with your gun or bow ready. You may need to shoot again. Stunned animals and even those mortally wounded have gotten up or thrashed around and injured hunters. Approach slowly and carefully, then touch the eyeball with your rifle muzzle or a stick. If the animal doesn't move, unload your gun or case your arrow and set aside. Then tag the animal with the appropriate tag or license.

Stop, take a breather, and relax a bit. The steps you take next will ensure your deer will turn into delicious venison your entire family will enjoy.

# 2. COMMON FALLACIES ABOUT DEER DRESSING

There are several fallacies that are quite common about dressing deer. Some have been touted for years as necessary to prevent the tainting of the meat. In fact, some may cause more problems than they alleviate.

The first is bleeding the animal. For years many writers suggested that the animal should be bled in the manner of pork and beef. That simply isn't true. Pork and beef are killed by a blow to the head or a low-power pellet in the brain and don't bleed at death. For that reason their throat must be cut and the blood allowed to escape from the body to prevent tainting of the meat by blood.

Deer are killed by either gunshot or arrow wounds that cause the animal to die from loss of blood, and there is no further need to bleed the animal. In fact, cutting into the throat and chest to bleed the animal allows more meat to be exposed to dirt, hair, flies, and so forth.

The second fallacy is that the scent glands must be removed from a buck because the strong odor will taint the meat. These glands are located on the hocks and are not apt to touch any of the meat during field dressing. The best approach is to leave them alone. If you remove the glands you'll get the scent on your knife blade and that will cause problems as it contacts the meat.

# 3. FIELD DRESSING

## EQUIPMENT

Although a number of excellent hunting knives can be used for field dressing, skinning, and butchering deer, there is actually no one knife that does all the jobs properly. A typical hunting knife can be used for field dressing, but a variety of butcher knives make the jobs of skinning and butchering much easier.

Actually, a pair of knives makes even field dressing much easier. A small skinning knife (maybe with a gut hook) will do most of the job, but a thick-bladed knife will split the breastbone more easily. Or you may prefer to carry a small hatchet or game saw for this task. Regardless of your choice in knives, be sure to purchase good quality, brand-name equipment and

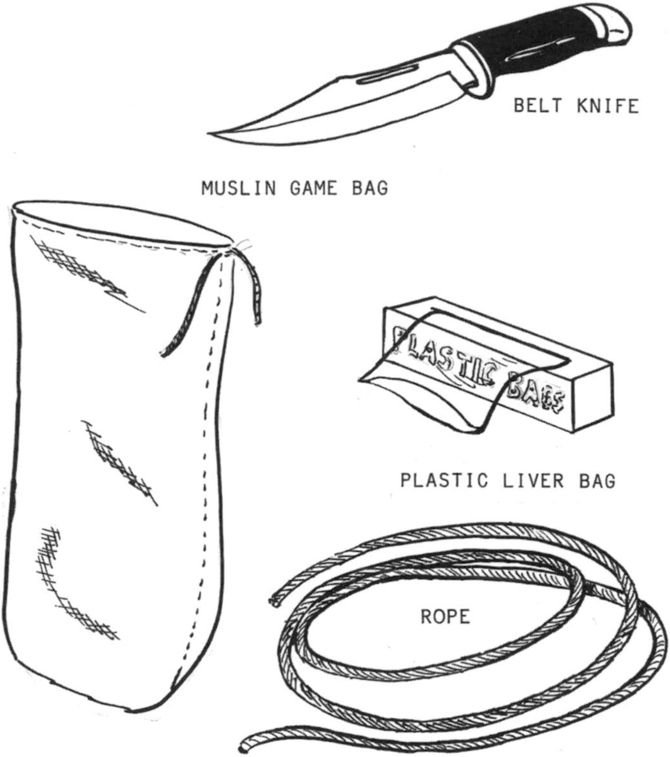

BELT KNIFE

MUSLIN GAME BAG

PLASTIC LIVER BAG

ROPE

keep them as sharp as possible. Dull knives require more force when cutting and that extra force can cause slipping and an accident.

A 15- to 20-foot section of rope can be invaluable for dragging out deer or hanging the animal in the woods or in camp. A tow strap to which the rope can be fastened can also be valuable in dragging out the carcass. A small block and tackle that can be carried in a backpack can also be valuable to hang the deer in the woods or at camp.

A large, self-closing, plastic kitchen bag should be used to transport the liver and heart from the woods.

You may also wish to use disposable plastic gloves for the field dressing chore. The long-sleeved variety used by veterinarians and farmers are excellent for the task and are available at many sporting goods stores and farm supply stores.

In hot weather, you should cover the deer with a cheesecloth game bag to keep away flies. Game bags can be purchased or you can make your own.

## STEPS TO FIELD DRESSING

If the animal can be transported to home or camp within half an hour, and the weather is cool (below 45 degrees), you may be better off field dressing the animal after transporting. This prevents dirt entering the carcass while dragging the gutted animal through the woods.

If, however, the weather is warm or it will take some time to get the carcass out of the woods, it should be field dressed immediately. Although not particularly hard, field dressing should be done properly or it can affect the meat.

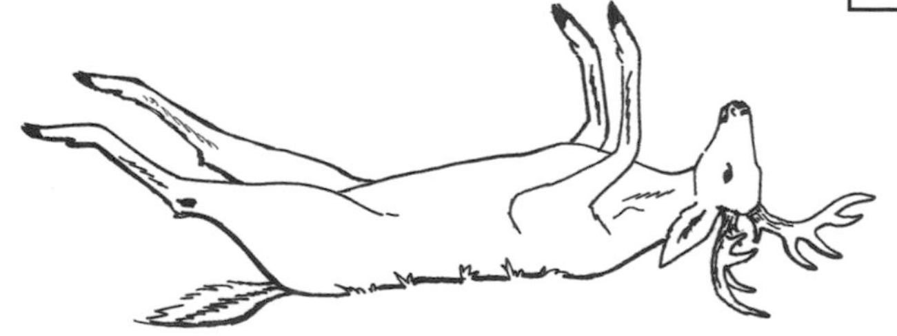

1. Roll the deer over on its back on a flat, smooth surface. If possible, have the head slightly higher than the rest of the body.

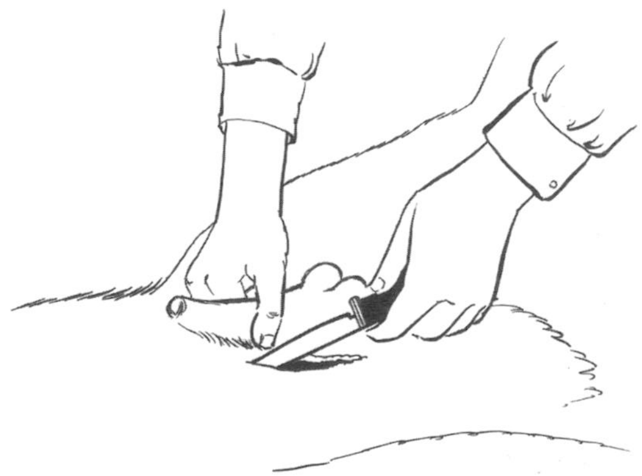

2. Make a shallow, 2- to 3-inch-long cut to one side of the penis if a buck or the udder if a doe. You

may wish to remove a buck's penis and scrotum at this time if allowed by law. (Check local laws—some require the genitals to remain on field dressed deer.) If removing, slice away from the skin and let the genitals hang back over the anus. Do not cut them away from the rest of the viscera at this time.

3. You're now ready to open the lower body area of the animal, and this must also be done properly—from the inside. Slicing from the outside of the skin will not only slice through hair and get it all over the meat, but may also let you slice through the paunch or intestines and spill waste on the meat. Stand straddling the animal and facing toward the head, then . . .

4. Extend the index and second finger of your hand, palm up, into the shallow cut made in the muscle and skin of the belly. Position the blade with the edge up between your two fingers and very carefully slit the belly muscle and skin all the way to the sternum of the rib cage or to where the last or bottom ribs join. This cut is the trickiest part of field dressing.

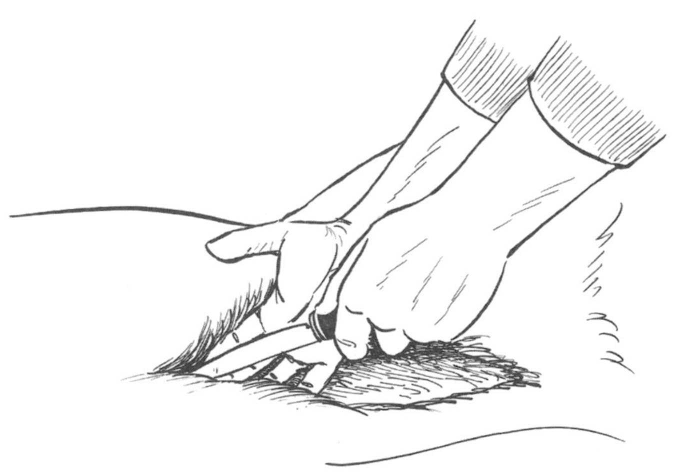

Keep pushing the paunch and intestines away with your fingers as you push the knife forward with your opposite hand and very carefully make the cut. Make sure

the knife point doesn't protrude too deeply and cut the paunch or stomach. As you make the cut, the entrails will start to bulge out of the body cavity.

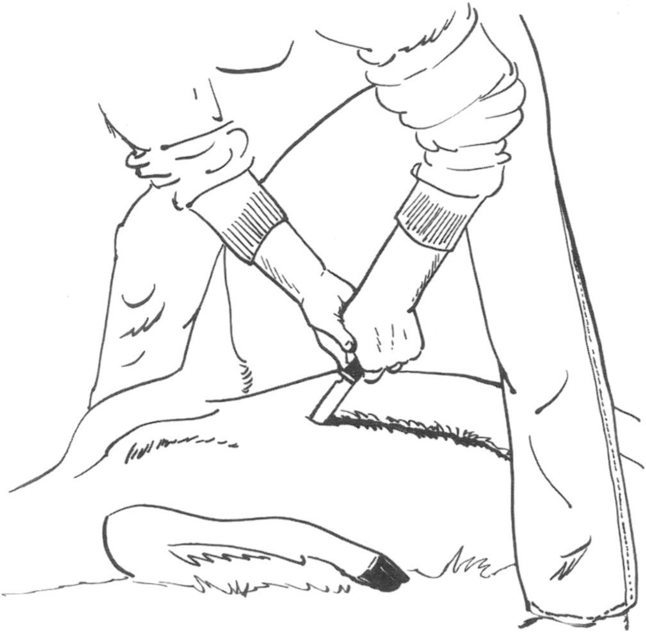

5. Next, cut through the rib cage to the neck of the animal. There are two methods to use depending on the equipment at hand. The first method is to continue slicing with the knife through the ribs toward the throat. The sternum or center of the rib cage on most deer is made of tough cartilage and not particularly hard. You may be able to slice through both skin and cartilage with a heavy-bladed knife,

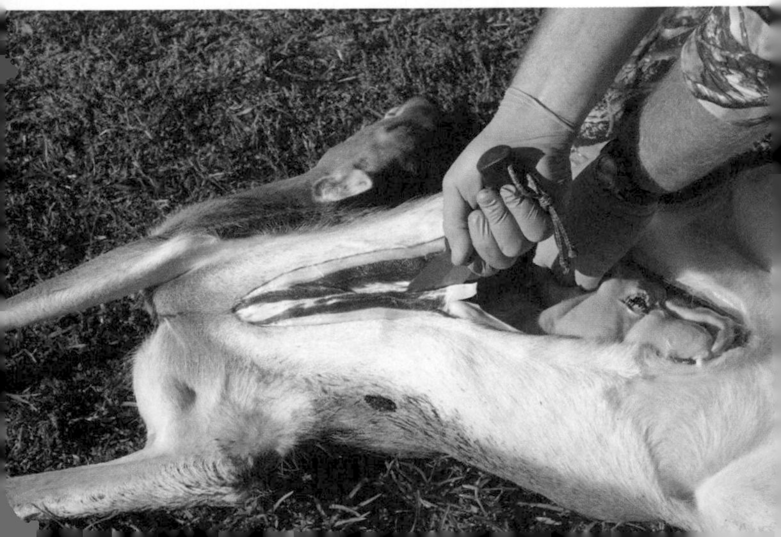

but it takes pressure. A heavy-bladed knife or axe can also be used to chop through the center of the rib cage. The simplest method is to hold the knife in position and strike the back of the knife with an axe head to force the knife through the cartilage and ribs. Or you can use a packable meat saw for the same purpose. After cutting through the ribs, continue slicing through the neck up to the jaw (unless the buck is a trophy you wish to have mounted). In this case, stop the cut below the brisket line. (For more information on caping trophy animals, refer to the chapter on caping.)

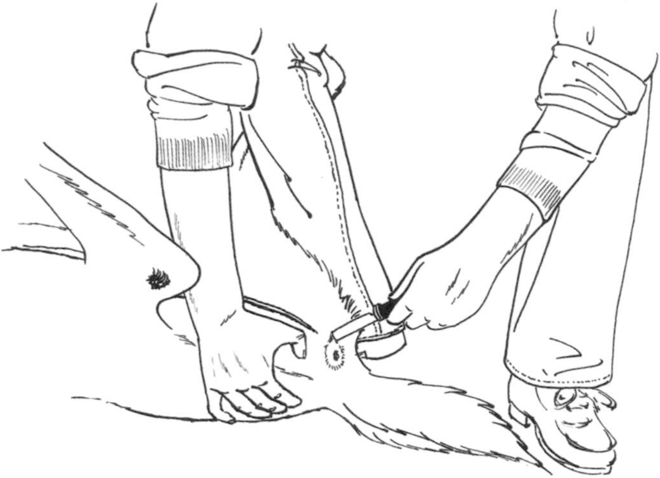

6. Move to the rear of the animal. With the point of a knife blade, make a cut completely encircling the rectum (or vaginal opening of a doe). Push the knife into the pelvic opening and cut around the anus, much like coring an apple. Then pull the rectum piece outside the body and tie off with a string. This prevents any feces

from being forced out during the rest of the field dressing. You now have two choices depending on the equipment available: you can push the tied-off rectum back through the pelvic arch into the body cavity or you can cut the pelvic arch and remove the rectum tubes through the opening.

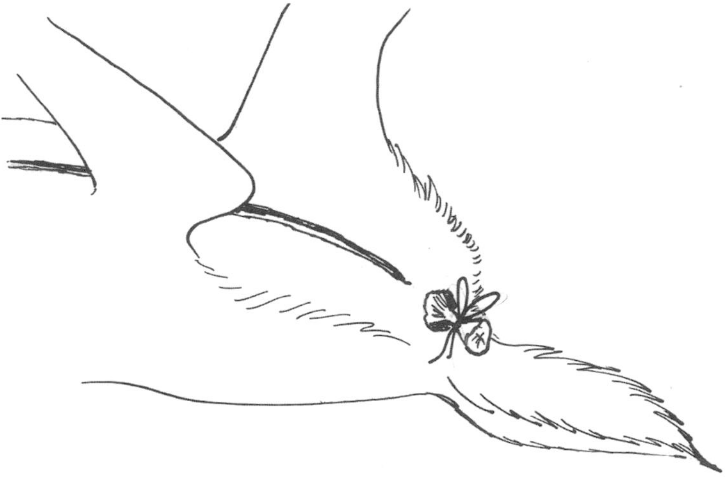

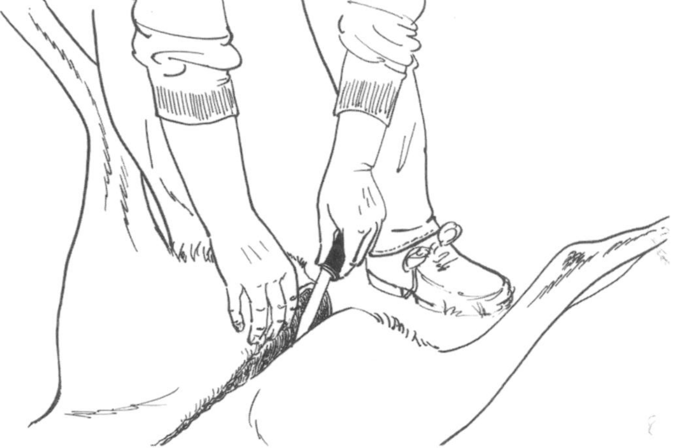

The simplest method is to split the pelvic arch. This can be done with a hatchet or heavy-bladed knife or by pounding on the back of your knife blade with a rock. Just don't ruin your knife. The cut can also be done with a small knife if you locate the white line in the exact center of the arch. Pressure at this point will cut through the arch on most deer, but will also dull a sharp knife.

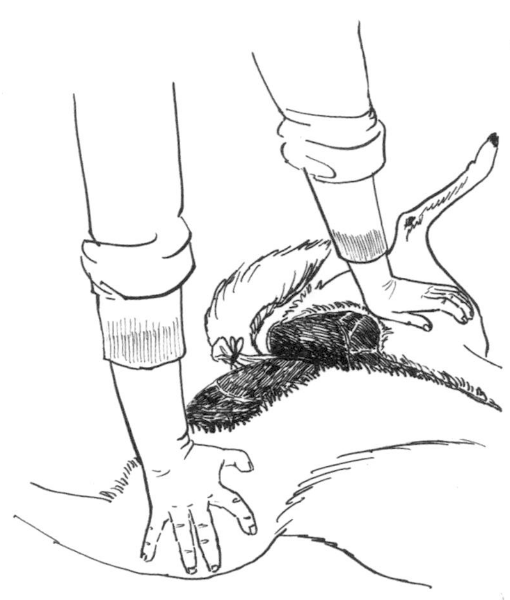

7. After cutting through the arch, push down on both legs. You will hear a snap when the arch breaks, leaving an open channel between the arch. Grasp the string-tied anus and pull the entire viscera, including the genitals, through the pelvic arch. In most instances you will need to cut to release the tubes from the body wall.

LOCATING THE ORGANS

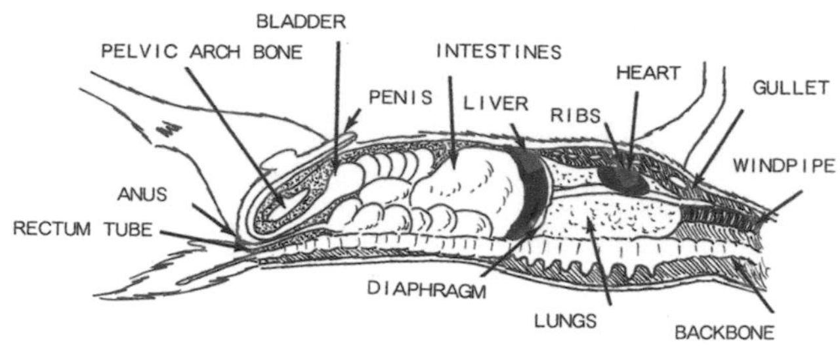


8. At this point the entire lower body portion of the viscera is ready to be removed. Step to the head of the animal, grasp the gullet (pushing the material in it forward), and then cut off the gullet and windpipe. Some hunters tie off this area before making the cut in the same manner as the rectum, but this isn't necessary. Cut around the diaphragm to allow the lungs and other organs in the rib cage to fall out. The rest is easy—turn

the carcass on its side and the intestines and paunch will roll out.

9. Cut away the liver, being extra careful not to cut into the bile (a dark greenish sac attached to the liver). Remove the heart and place both in a plastic bag.

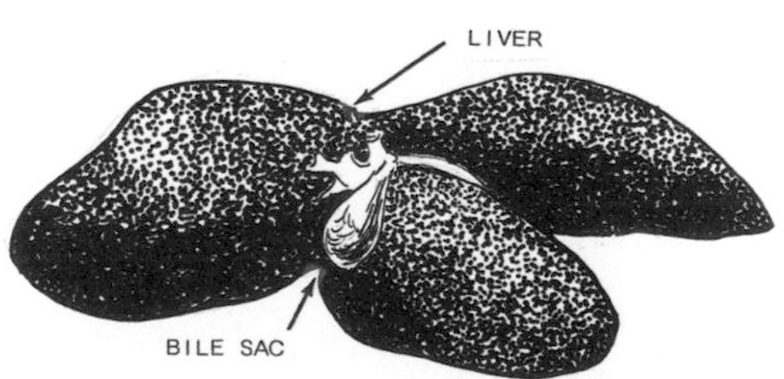

10. If you have water nearby, wash the blood from inside the body cavity. If not, wipe with cloth or paper towels.
11. If the weather is cool and it will be some time before you get back to the animal, prop open the chest cavity with a stick to provide the fastest cooling possible. If the weather is warm, leave the cavity closed to prevent fly damage.

With practice, field dressing can be quick and simple.

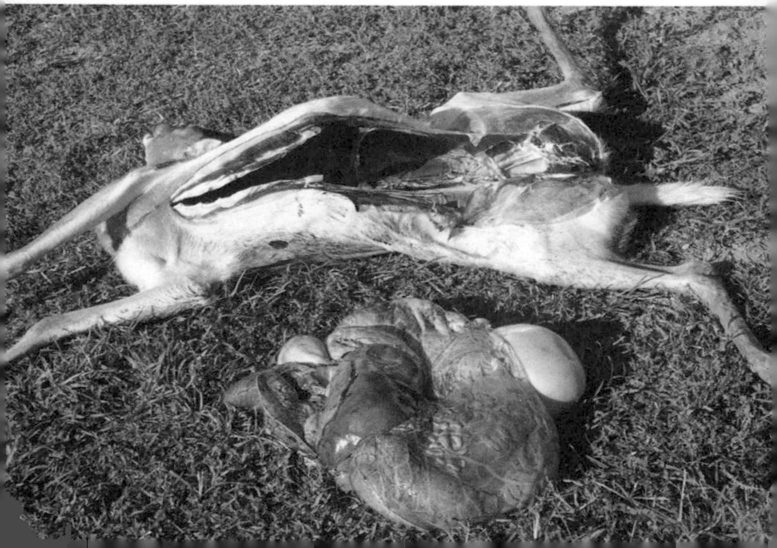

12. Move the entrails some distance away from the carcass and you're ready to drag out your deer. If you intend to get help, mark the spot well so you can find it again or take good visual readings if you're afraid someone will steal your kill. This happens all too frequently on public lands.

# 4. TRANSPORTING

The picture of early frontiersmen carrying a deer slung over their shoulder is quite romantic, but it's not the best method of transporting a deer. The average whitetail today is quite a bit heftier than their ancestors thanks to a wider variety of protein-rich foods.

The best method for short hauls is to drag the deer home. This works quite well for downhill or flat land. When it comes to dragging a deer over a western mountain, you may decide to quarter it first and pack it out. Again, that is subject to local law.

Most bucks are simply dragged by their horns out of the woods, and this is still the simplest but hardest method of transportation. A dead deer is not easy to drag. You can simplify the chore by

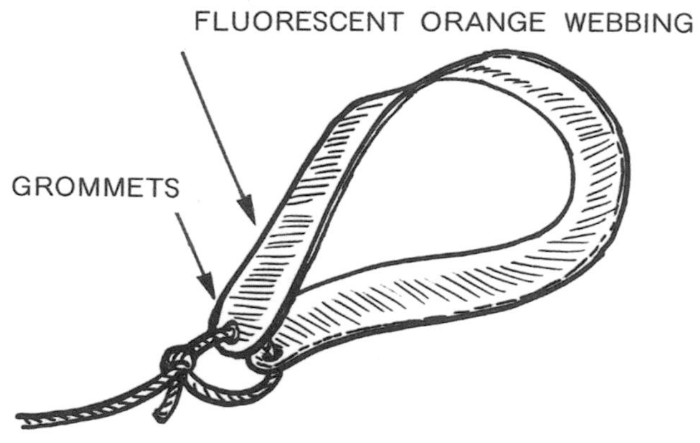


using a haul rope. Tie the front legs to the head, looping the rope around the head and legs and the other end of the rope over your shoulders. A homemade haul strap of blaze orange material can further simplify the hauling chore. Looped over your shoulders, the strap prevents rope burns. Two hunters with two tow ropes and harnesses pulling about five feet apart can make the job of dragging even the biggest deer much easier.

Two hunters can carry a field-dressed buck out on a sapling. Tie the feet together and run the sapling through them. The swinging dead weight is still a difficult haul. A travois can also be rigged out of two saplings.

In many instances the carcass can be transported by vehicle. One of the biggest mistakes made, however, is tying the animal to the hood of your vehicle. Not only is the carcass subject to road dust, heat, and drying wind, but also the heat of the motor, all of which can affect the meat quality.

The best bet is to place the carcass inside the car trunk with the lid left partially open, the back of a pick-up, or inside a station wagon. If using a station wagon or suv, leave the windows open to allow for air circulation and don't use the

heater. If you have some distance to drive, place a bag of ice inside the body cavity to help cool.

A four-wheeler with a rack makes getting your deer out of the woods easy.

# 5. HANGING

The carcass should be hung to cool and to keep from predators. This can be done using a rope with a half-hitch around the horns, the rope thrown over a limb, and then the animal pulled up. It's hard work

even with a small deer. A small block and tackle can make the job four times easier. If the weather is warmer than 45 degrees, pull a game bag over the carcass.

In most instances, the carcass will be hung at camp or home. Ideally, the carcass should hang for a week to ten days at 40 to 45 degrees to age properly. If weather conditions permit, you can produce venison that will rival the best beef you have ever tasted. Young deer don't require as much aging—some can be cut up in a day or two. Older bucks require the most aging.

Deer killed in hot weather, such as early bow season, must be skinned and butchered immediately; however, the meat will taste strong and be tougher than if allowed to hang and age properly. Another method to age meat when necessary is in an old refrigerator. Set the refrigerator to 45 degrees and cut the carcass into pieces that will fit. Keep the meat in the refrigerator for a couple

of weeks. Small deer can be quartered, but larger deer must be cut into smaller pieces—it's best to bone out all of the less desirable pieces such as ribs, shanks, and so forth. The meat will also need to be turned to prevent one side sitting in blood. If the nights are cool, move the pieces to a table on an enclosed porch or other cool room. Be sure to keep all meat covered and protected.

It's harder to age the small trim pieces in this manner as they continue to drain blood. If left to sit in blood for any length of time, they can become slimy. For that reason, small trim pieces should be ground into sausage or wrapped for stew meat fairly quickly.

Hang the deer in a cool, dry place. If this is on a meat pole or big limb outdoors, leave the hide on. If the deer can be hung in a cool garage or other enclosed building, you may prefer to skin the animal. Skinning allows the meat to cool faster, and a thin, hard coating will

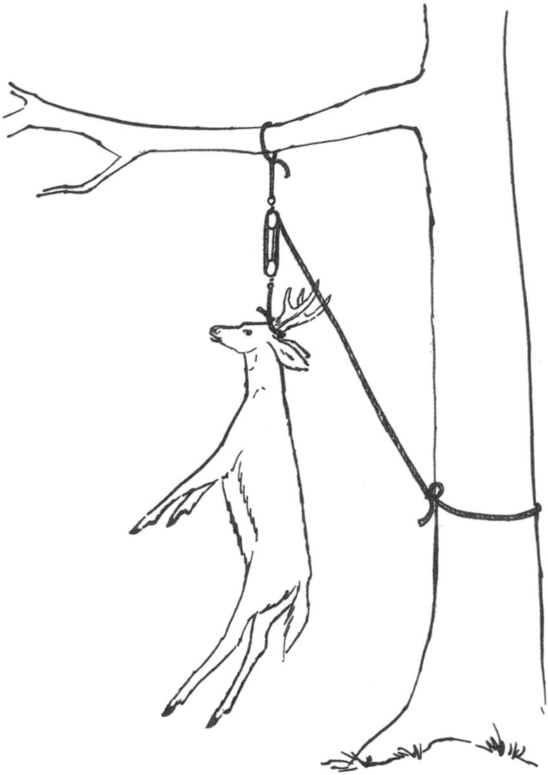

The field-dressed carcass should be hung and allowed to cool down, temperature permitting.

quickly form over the entire carcass. This will protect the meat and provide the best aging process.

The carcass can be hung head down or by the head. If the skin is to be left on, hang by the antlers or head. If the skin is removed, hang by the back legs. I prefer to hang by the back legs for another reason: any blood in the head and throat won't continue to drain down into the body cavity.

If the deer is a trophy that you wish to have mounted, hang by the back legs to remove the head and cape as instructed in chapter 7 on caping.

Regardless of which method is used you must have a good solid support to hold the animal. The support can be a meat pole erected at home or camp, a solid tree limb, or cross bracing in a garage, barn, or so forth. If hung outside, the lowest portion of the animal should be well out of reach of predators, including cats and dogs. Cats can be one of the worst problems.

## HANGING BY THE BACK LEGS

You will need two pieces of equipment. First, a gambrel or spreader positioned between the hocks to spread the body and hold it open. The gambrel can be made of a stout piece of sapling such as hickory or oak, with the ends sharpened as shown. A gambrel can also be made up from a piece of steel reinforcing rod, welding to size and shape.

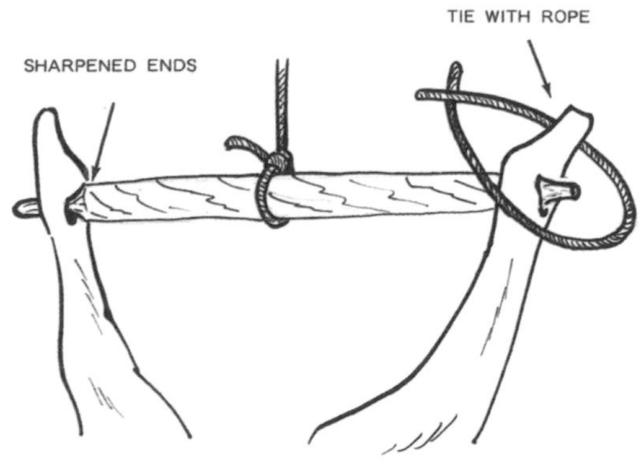

## HANGING AND SKINNING TOOLS

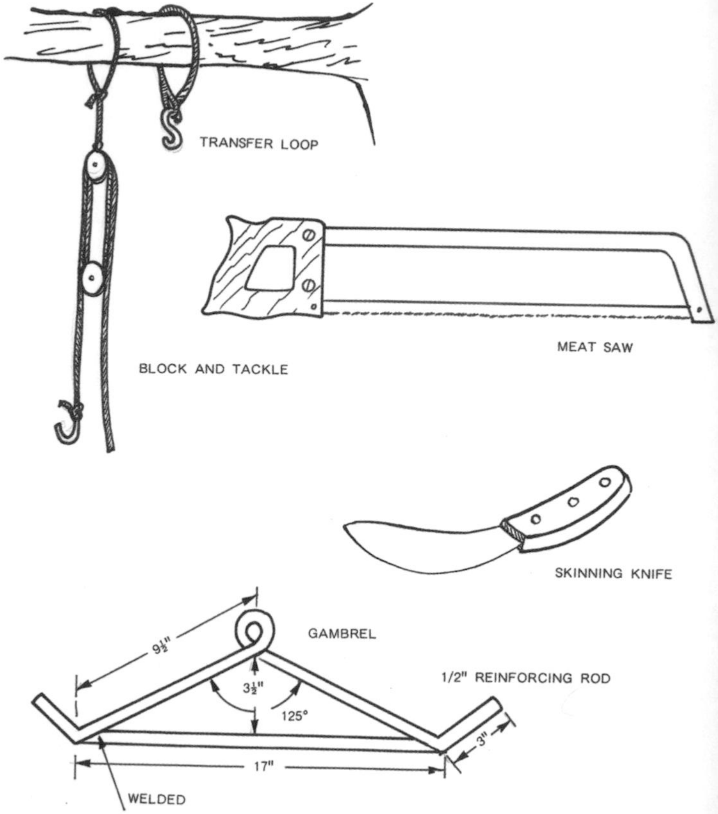

TRANSFER LOOP

MEAT SAW

BLOCK AND TACKLE

SKINNING KNIFE

GAMBREL

9½"

1/2" REINFORCING ROD

3½"

125°

3"

17"

WELDED

The second piece of equipment is a transfer loop that is secured to the meat pole. The carcass is raised into position, then the eye hook of the transfer loop is placed in the gambrel hook and the block and tackle removed. Or you may wish to keep the deer attached to the block and tackle for easier skinning.

To hang with the skin on, saw off the back legs just below the hocks. Or you can leave them on, which I normally do. Insert the point of a knife from the side opposite the scent glands and make a cut that will just allow the ends of the gambrel to slip in place. If using the wooden gambrel, secure with thongs. Pull the deer up into position and tie off the rope or secure with a transfer loop. Again, add spreaders to the body cavity to open it as much as possible.

## HANGING BY THE HEAD

Make a half-hitch loop around the horns, secure a knot, and hook the block and tackle in place. Pull the deer up until the lower feet clear the ground. Cut spreaders of limbs or pieces of wood and spread the chest cavity as open as possible to allow for good air circulation and drainage. Raise the carcass as high as possible.

## REMOVING DELICACIES

In addition to the liver and heart, other delicacies should be removed. The tenderloins are inside the carcass next to the rib cage on either side of the backbone. If they are not removed, they will dry hard and shrivel up during aging. The tenderloins can be pulled out quite easily by inserting your finger underneath them on the upper end or forward part. Pull and use a knife to help cut them away. The kidneys are also located on each side

of the backbone and can also be easily pulled out.

## CARING FOR DELICACIES

The heart and liver should soak in several changes of water. Then hang the liver in a safe place to drain for a bit. Slice and prepare your first venison meal of liver. Package and freeze the rest.

Kidneys should be washed in several changes of water and allowed to drain and dry. They are best if cooked immediately.

Tenderloin is ready to eat immediately or can be frozen.

# 6. SKINNING

The hardest task in skinning is keeping loose hairs off the meat. Always cut through the skin from the underside, and avoid cutting through the hairs. Pick off any loose hairs as they appear.

Regardless of how you hang the animal, the best position for skinning is head down. If you plan to hang the carcass without the skin, starting the skinning is much easier while the animal is still on the ground. Then gradually raise the animal up as you skin. That way, you don't need to reach high or low for the chore.

A game hoist can make skinning and butchering much simpler and easier. It allows you to raise and lower the carcass as needed so you aren't bending over or reaching high. Start with the carcass

high and do the front legs, then lower the carcass and begin skinning on the back legs. Raise the carcass as you skin downward.

1. Make a cut to insert the gambrel between the tendon and bone on each hind leg.

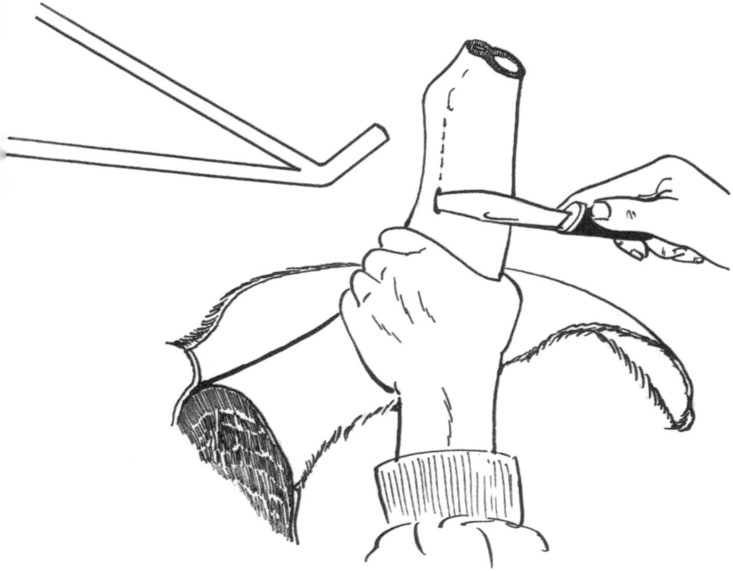

2. Insert the gambrel in place and hoist the carcass off the ground.

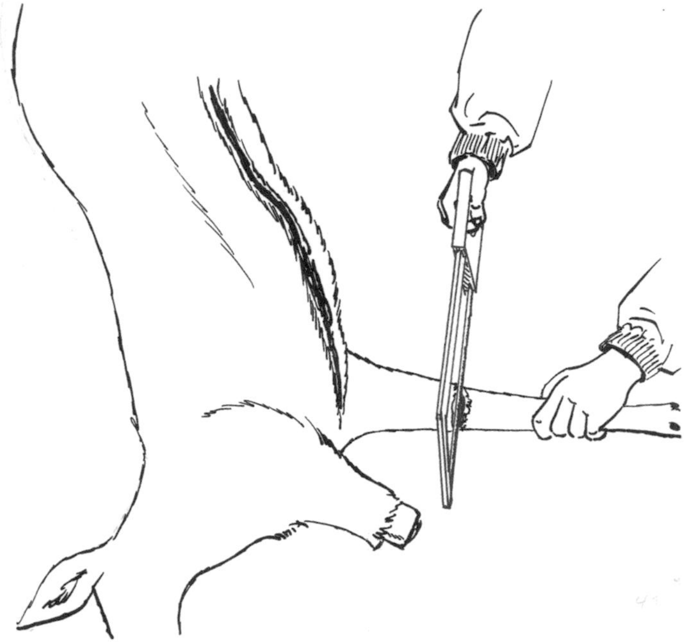

3. Using the meat saw, cut off the front legs.

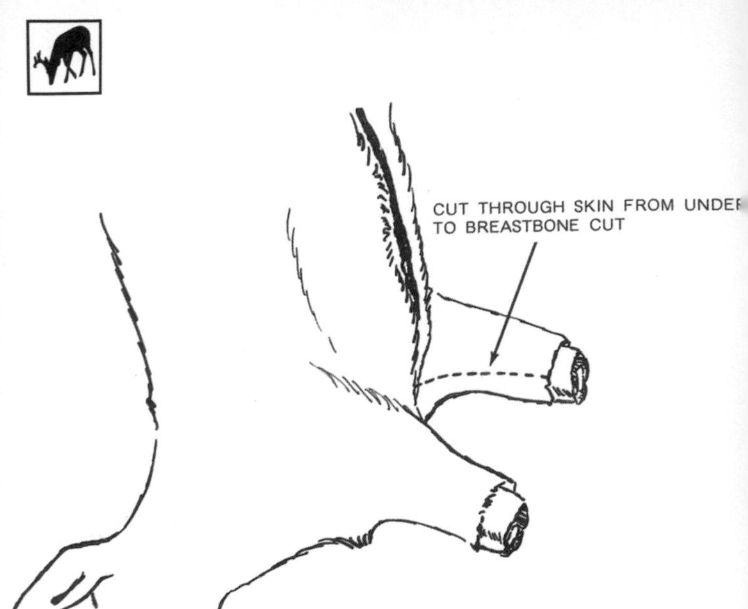


4. Make a cut in the skin on the inside legs from the chest cut to the ends of the sawed off legs and skin out the front legs back to the shoulder. The reason for this is as the hide is peeled off, it drapes down around the front legs and makes working on them somewhat awkward.

5. Lower the animal so you have a good working height. Starting at the rump, skin out the thighs and rump. Start with a slit in the skin from the pelvic cut to the sawed end on each hind leg. Cut from the underneath side of the skin to prevent cutting through hairs and getting them on the meat.

   Once you get a good start on the skin, you can usually "fist" or pull a great deal of the skin away from the muscle, using the knife only occasionally.

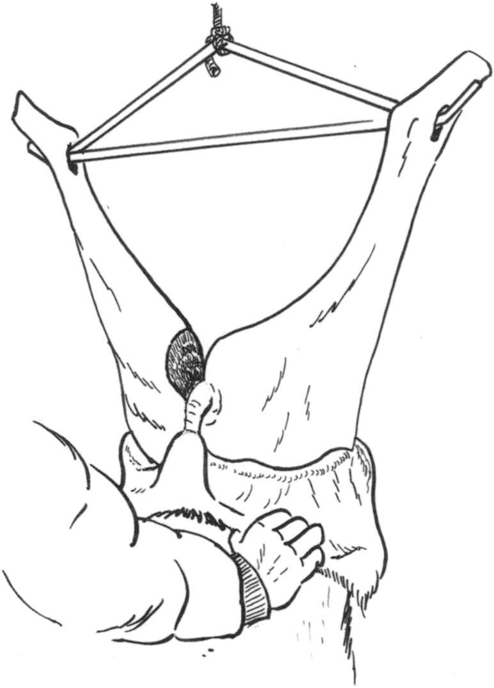

6. When you get to the tail, skin under and around it, peel the skin down over the tail an inch or so, and then saw the tail off close to the body.

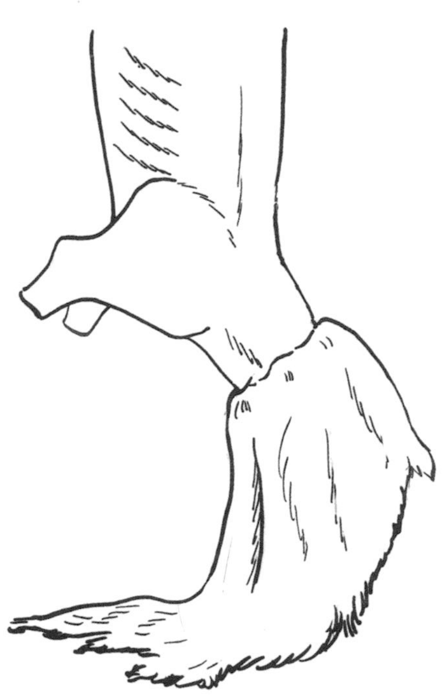

7. Once you get down over the rump, the skin will peel off fairly easily. Pull down with one hand and use the fleshing or skinning knife to cut the skin from the meat only where it sticks. This will be particularly so on the belly area.

8. Pull and cut the skin down to the joint of the neck and head, and then remove the head. Using a sharp knife, slice all around the neck at the junction of the jaw and neck and then twist the head to break the back bone. It takes just a little cutting then to sever the head.
9. Clean all hairs from the carcass.
10. Cut the head away from the hide and salt the hide liberally. Roll the hide up, hair side out, and take immediately to the tanner or taxidermist, or place in the freezer until you get a chance to do so.

# 7. CAPING

If you plan to have your trophy mounted, the skinning is done quite differently. In this case the head and cape is very carefully removed first. If the animal is a true trophy, all steps including field dressing should be altered so there are no cuts on the skin of the underside of the neck to behind the front legs, including during field dressing.

Caping consists of making a cut encircling the body just behind the tops of the shoulders and the front legs. Then cut down the inside of the front legs to just above the front joint. Make a cut encircling the leg, then make a cut from the top of the shoulders to the back of the neck to just behind the skull. Make a Y- or T-shaped cut across the back of the skull. Pull the cape back starting behind

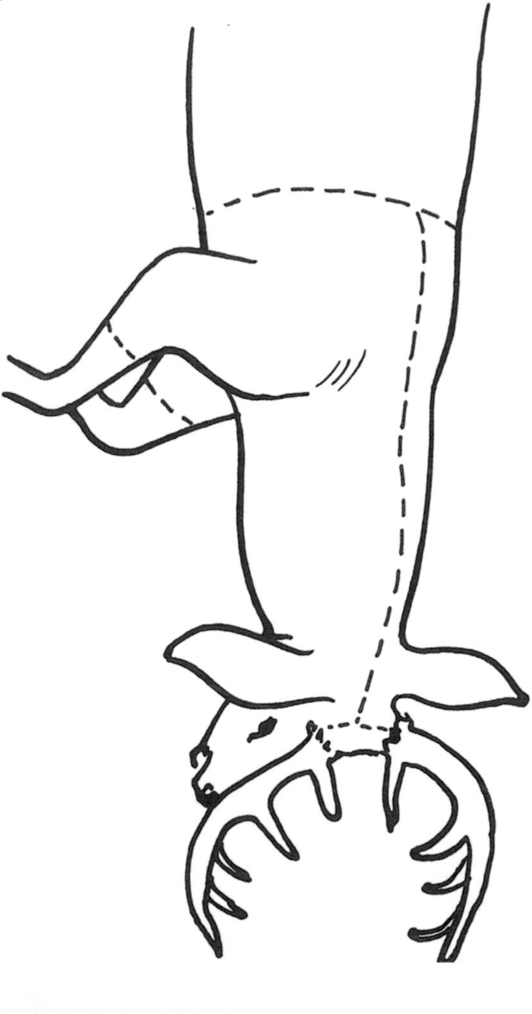

the shoulders, again using the knife only to loosen where needed.

When you get to the head, cut it off at the joint of the neck and head. If you can, get the head and cape to a taxidermist immediately, most taxidermists prefer the mount delivered in that manner. If not, freeze the cape and head.

# 8. BUTCHERING

After all the work of field dressing and skinning, butchering is an easy chore. Butchering your own meat does take some extra tools, but most will already be on hand from the field dressing and skinning. You will need a variety of butcher knives, including a large knife for slicing steaks and a thin-bladed boning knife to bone out meat. You may also wish to have a butcher's steel to help keep the knife edges sharp as you work. A few strokes on either side will make cutting chores much easier.

You will also need a meat saw. Scour the saw with hot soapy water with a little household bleach added, then rinse with clean hot water before using. Make sure the saw teeth are thoroughly cleaned.

An additional piece of equipment is a meat grinder. You don't need a heavy-duty industrial-type grinder; any kitchen meat grinder will do the job. To preserve your harvest you will need plastic food wrap or freezer bags and butcher paper or a vacuum sealing machine and the appropriate bags.

Cutting up the carcass of any animal requires a good clean working space. This can be a table setup in a shop, garage, barn, or outside if weather permits. If done in warm weather, try finding an area free of flies.

A clean working table can be made using 2x4s and sawhorse brackets. Make a pair of waist-high sawhorses and use clean planks for the top. This type of table can be folded or dismantled and easily stored until the next deer.

All equipment must be washed with hot soapy water (with a little household bleach added) and rinsed with clean hot water before and after use.

## CUTTING UP THE CARCASS

There are two methods of cutting up the carcass, depending on the meat cuts you prefer as well as the equipment available. Use a saw for the initial cuts and cut the carcass in the traditional manner, or you can simply use a boning knife and remove all the meat from the bones. The latter is the easiest to do, requires less equipment, and takes up much less freezer space. These days, I often completely bone out the carcass while still hanging and without using a meat saw. A combination of the two methods can also be used, utilizing the best of each.

Regardless of which method you use, you'll find that cutting up the meat is a pleasant, easy task and even if you don't cut it up correctly (according to purchased beef cuts), it will all cook so you really can't go wrong.

# CUTTING THE CARCASS IN HALF

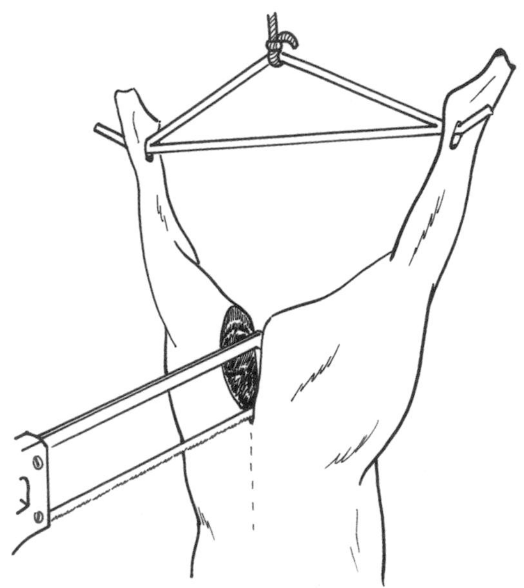

1. With the carcass suspended by the hocks, use the meat saw to split the carcass in half down the centerline of the back bone, starting at the point where the tail was removed. Slicing the muscle down to the bone with a knife will reveal

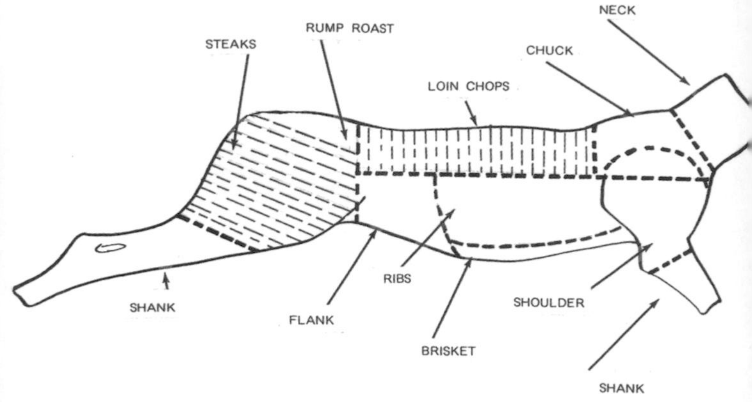


the centerline starting point. Saw straight down the center of the back bone and through the neck.

2. Lay the two carcass halves down on the work surface. Shown is a drawing of the typical cuts that can be made on each half. Follow these for traditional meat cuts or cut off whatever you desire, boning some or all.

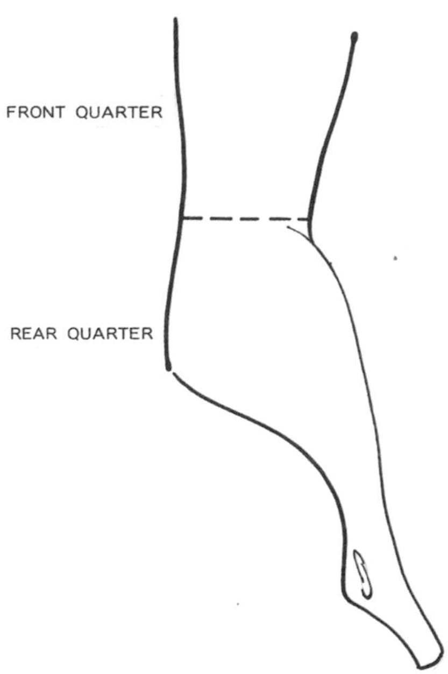


3. Remove the hind quarter from the front quarter by cutting on a line parallel to the front muscle of the leg. This cut should first be made through the muscle on the front and back with a knife, then complete the cut with a saw.

# CUTTING THE HIND QUARTER

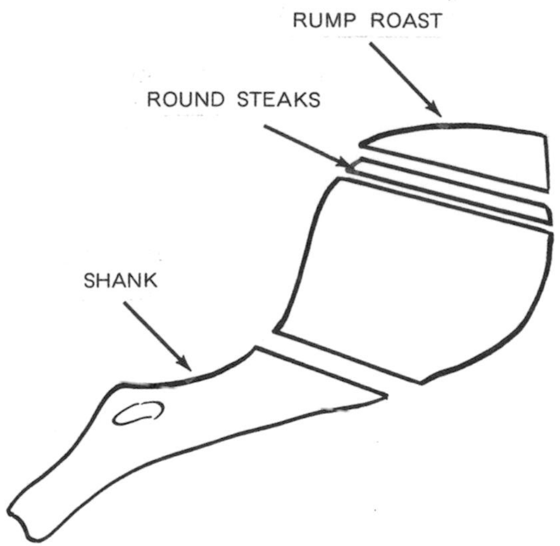


1. The top of the hind quarter can be cut to produce a rump roast by cutting across the top at an angle as shown. The shank can then be cut off and the rest of the leg sliced into round steaks.
2. Slice off the steaks and then cut through the bone with a saw for

each steak. The easiest method is to bone the meat from the joint first, then slice the chunks into steaks.

3. Roll the boned section of meat into a paper package and place on a pan in the freezer. Leave in the freezer just long enough to cool the meat down to 36 or 38 degrees; the meat handles and slices much easier at that temperature. Then slice the steaks into the desired thickness. You may also wish to lightly pound the steaks with a meat mallet before wrapping for the freezer.
4. Bone out the shank portion, trim out all the sinew and gristle, and cut into 1-inch chunks for either grinding or stew meat. Keep these pieces in the refrigerator until you are ready to grind all the meat or package as stew meat.

## CUTTING THE FRONT SHOULDER

1. The front shoulder is removed from the carcass by slicing directly between the leg and brisket and slicing toward the top or back of the animal. Lift up as you slice and the leg will come off easily. The front leg doesn't fit into a socket as the rear leg does.

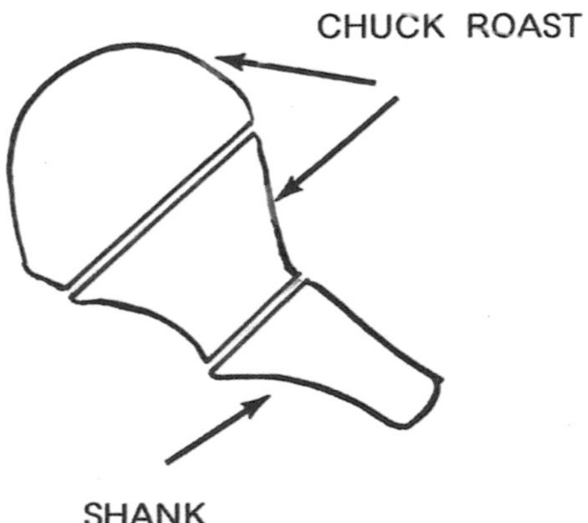

2. Remove the shank piece as shown, using a saw. Then the shoulder can be sawn into two separate chuck roast pieces and the shank can again be trimmed for stew meat or deerburger. Note: There isn't a lot of meat on the shoulder and it can be somewhat tough. You may wish to bone the entire shoulder and grind it into burger.
3. The neck is removed by cutting through the muscle with a knife, then completing the cut with a saw. Bone all meat away from the bone and add to the stew or ground meat.

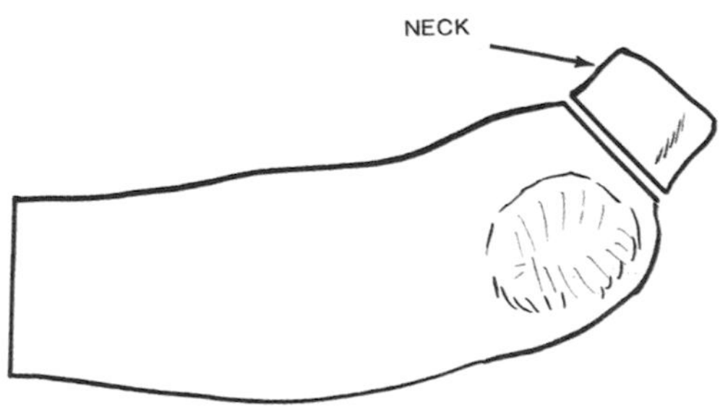

# CUTTING THE SIDE

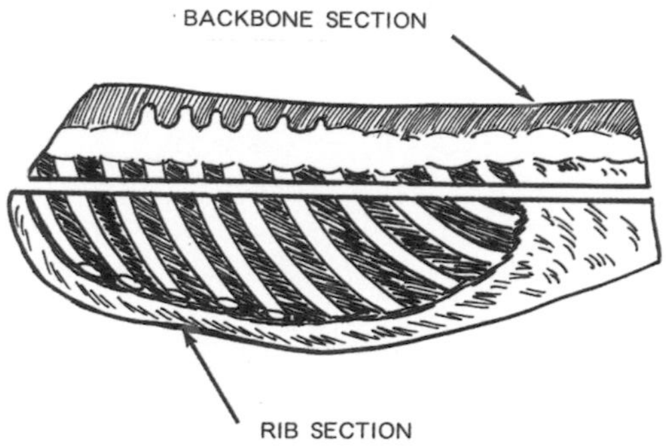


The side can be cut into ribs and deer chops or you can bone out the entire side. Slice up the boned loin into steaks or create a boneless loin roast, which is great smoked. All scrap pieces would, of course, go into the stew meat or deerburger. This is the easiest method and good for quick, hot weather butchering. Very little meat is found on venison ribs.

The carcass sides can also be made into more traditional pieces similar to beef:

1. Saw the side across the ribs starting at the front of the carcass and making the cut where the meat starts to thicken on the ribs. This is usually about one-third of the way down from the top of the back.

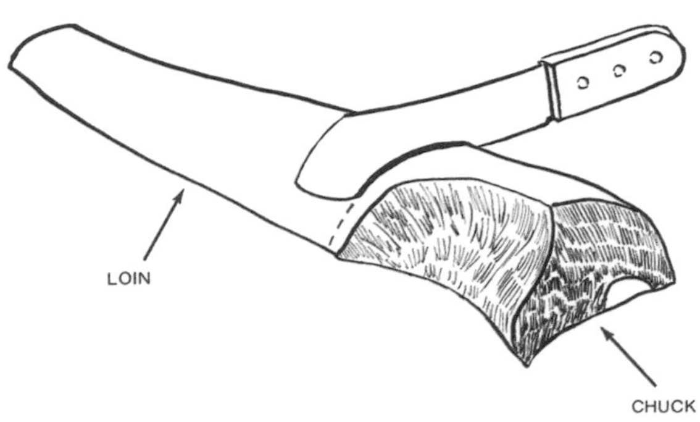


2. Cut the front portion (from where the shoulder joined) from the rest of the backbone section. This can also be divided into two chuck pieces or boned and cut into stew or ground meat.

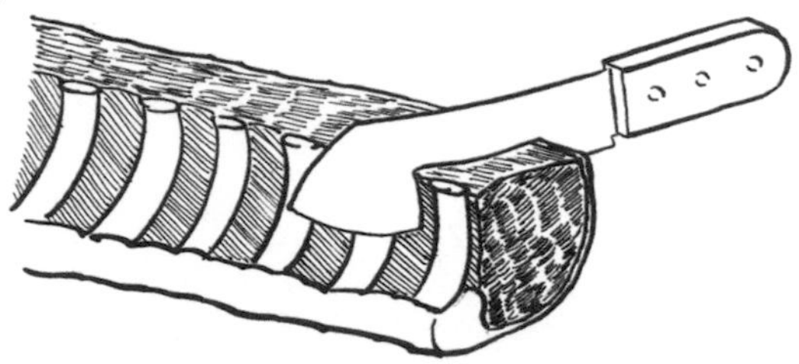

3. The loin section can then be cut into chops, making them as thick as you desire. Start the cuts with a knife and then finish through the backbone and ribs with a meat saw.
4. Trim the brisket and flank from the ribs and add them to the stew or ground meat.
5. Separate ribs using a sharp knife, slicing between them and pulling apart.

At this point one side is cut and ready to be wrapped and frozen. You can either stop and wrap those pieces or cut up the other side and then wrap all the pieces at the same time.

## TRIMMING FAT

One of the biggest problems with venison is the fat can become quite rancid. Trim all fat away from the meat, and also trim as much sinew, gristle, and tough pieces as well. Trim all cuts before freezing, as well as all meat to be ground. It is especially important to remove the sinew from all meat to be ground as the sinew makes the meat harder to grind.

# 9. DEERBURGER

All the tougher cuts of meat, small trimmings from boning, and so forth can be ground with a meat grinder to produce deerburger. You will end up with all lean meat that is excellent for chili, tacos, and almost any other recipe calling for ground meat. However, if you wish to fry or grill burgers, you will need to grind in a bit of beef suet. The venison can also be ground with pork, but the mixture won't keep as long in the freezer. The lean ground venison can also be mixed with fresh ground pork when ready to make into patties or a loaf. Wear rubber gloves while handling and grinding meat for burger.

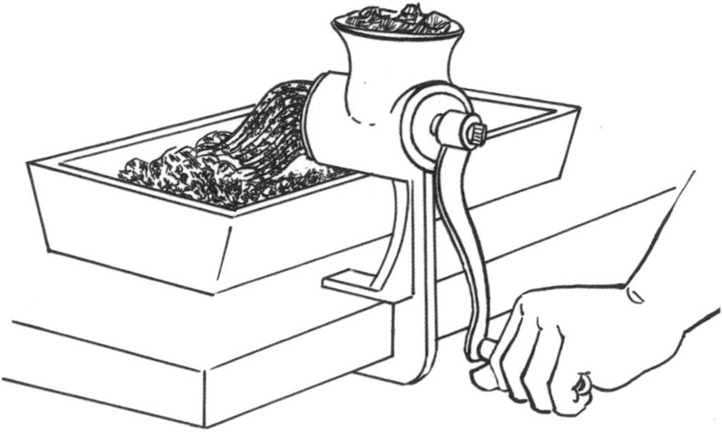

A hand grinder can be used for grinding venison, but a power grinder makes the chore much quicker and easier.

# 10. WRAPPING AND FREEZING

All cuts should be double wrapped—first in plastic wrap or a sealing plastic bag and then butcher paper or in vacuum sealed bags. Be sure to label each package as to the cut, number of servings, date, and so forth. Place in the fast-freeze section of your deep freeze immediately.

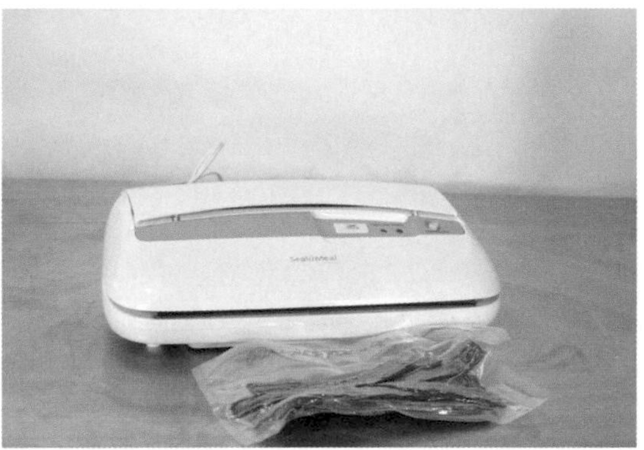

You can extend the storage time of your venison, including jerky, by using a vacuum packer.

# 11. COOKING VENISON

As with any meat, a young animal provides the most tender and best-tasting food.

The taste of the venison you serve depends a great deal on the care taken after your deer was shot and the age of the animal. Even an older animal that has hung properly and is cooked accordingly will make delicious eating. Also remember that tough cuts of beef will also be tough in venison and will need to be prepared accordingly.

Venison should always be served hot. When the fat congeals on cold venison, it turns rancid. Always trim away as much fat as possible while butchering. Venison should be served well-done to prevent the possibility of trichinosis; however, the meat is also very dry and can easily be overcooked.

## TENDERLOIN AND LOIN OR CHOPS

The tenderloin on almost any age deer will be tender enough to fry or grill. The

loin or chops on most animals will also be tender enough to prepare as desired.

Our favorite methods are to slice the meat, pound salt, pepper, and flour into both sides, and brown in an iron skillet with a little oil or marinate slices in teriyaki marinade and grill.

## STEAK

Steaks from young deer or properly aged older deer can be prepared in the same manner as the loins. If more tenderizing is needed, fry as above, place in a baking dish, cover with gravy, canned soup, or tomato sauce (with onions and green peppers added), and bake until fork tender.

## DEER ROAST

The two small rump roasts on a deer are the only roasts that can be prepared in the traditional manner. We grind the front shoulder or chuck into burger.

The rump roast should be covered with sliced onions and strips of bacon, then tightly wrapped in foil and baked.

## RIBS

Venison ribs are rather dry and have very little meat on them, making them difficult to prepare like pork ribs. They can, however, be used as deer chops or a standing rib roast.

# 12. A FEW RECIPES

## VENISON TACOS

Brown one pound ground venison along with one diced onion and one diced green pepper. When the meat is cooked and the vegetables tender, stir in one can refried beans and one package taco seasoning. Add some salsa or taco sauce if mixture is too dry. Serve this mixture in taco or burrito shells or over tortilla chips for a taco salad. Add shredded cheese, diced onion, and tomatoes and shredded lettuce along with the sauce of your choice and sour cream.

## MAPLE-FLAVORED BREAKFAST VENISON SAUSAGE

Mix together one pound ground venison with one pound ground pork (not sausage, plain ground pork). When the meats are well mixed, add 1 tablespoon salt, 2 heaping tablespoons brown sugar, 1 teaspoon ground black pepper, ¼ teaspoon (or to taste) crushed red pepper, and ¼ teaspoon maple flavoring. Blend in the seasonings by hand until well mixed. Make into sausage patties and fry in a skillet or bake at 350 degrees until cooked. These make great breakfast sandwiches.

## VENISON ROAST

Debone a venison rump roast and remove all fat and sinew. Rub the outside of the roast with garlic pepper (or a seasoning of your choice). Place in a slow cooker, add one package dry onion soup mix, two cups water, and one cup red wine. Cook on low for 8 hours or until tender, adding more liquid if needed.

# 13. VENISON JERKY

Jerky is one of our favorite venison foods and an excellent way of using up some of the tougher cuts. Jerky is easy to make and provides a nutritious and tasty snack.

Jerky made from venison, pork, or bear meat should first be frozen or thoroughly cooked to kill trichina. Trichina is a parasite that can give you trichinosis if it is not killed. Either precook the meat slices or freeze the meat at 0 degrees F before slicing.

Slice the meat with the grain into very thin, ⅛-inch strips. The meat will slice better if partially frozen. After slicing, remove all fat. Place the sliced meat in a bowl with a tight-fitting lid and pour the following marinade over it:

2 lbs. meat, thinly sliced
1 tbs. Worcestershire sauce
1 tbs. salt
½ tsp. black pepper
2 tbs. onion powder
1 tsp. garlic powder, or to taste
½ cup brown sugar
Tabasco sauce to taste

Cover the meat with cold water and place the tightly covered bowl in the refrigerator for one to two days. Shake or stir often. Then drain and pat dry the meat slices and dehydrate. Meats can be dried in a commercial dehydrator, solar powered units, or your gas or electric oven. Set the oven to the lowest possible temperature and leave the door ajar for circulation. Cheesecloth-covered wooden trays that will slide into your oven rack grooves make excellent oven-drying racks. You may also need a drip tray in the bottom of the oven.

Drying time for jerky will vary according to the thickness of the cut strips. Most jerky will oven dry in 6 to 7 hours. When dry, meat will be coal black and should bend but not break.

Store jerky in airtight containers kept in a cool, dry, dark location. Jerky will keep almost indefinitely in the freezer.

For more information about making jerky, see the author's *The Complete Jerky Book*, also available from this publisher.

# ABOUT THE AUTHORS

Monte Burch (left) and nephew Morgan Burch

Monte and Joan Burch live on a farm managed for wildlife in the heart of the Ozarks. Hunting, butchering, and preparing their own food has been a

way of life passed down to them from several generations. They learned from practical experience how to butcher and prepare for the table chickens, pigs, beef, and wildlife, including deer. They offer this knowledge in the hope that more hunters and their families will enjoy the delicious taste of properly butchered and prepared venison.

Monte is the author of over seventy books on the outdoors and how-to subjects and has been a regular contributor to most of the major outdoor magazines for almost fifty years.

# NOTES

# NOTES

# NOTES

# NOTES

# NOTES

# NOTES

# NOTES

# NOTES

# NOTES

# NOTES

# NOTES

# NOTES

# NOTES

# NOTES

# NOTES

# NOTES

# NOTES

# NOTES

# NOTES

# NOTES

# NOTES

# NOTES

# NOTES

# NOTES

# NOTES

# NOTES

# NOTES